# Dot's Poetry

## by

## Dot Osika

*D. Osika*

Open Door Publishers, Inc.
Malta, NY

*See,  I have placed*
*before you an open*
*door that no  one can shut.*
*Rev 3:8*

Open Door Publishers, Inc
P.O. Box 2871
Malta, NY 12020  (518) 899-2097
http://www.opendoorpublishers.com

Printed in the United States of America


First Edition

First Printing 2012

ISBN:  978-1-937138-13-4

## Dedication

I dedicate these words and ideas in this book of poetry

to my ever loving husband, Louis Osika

# Table of Contents

## A NON-Poet!

I'm not a poet and know it!
Yet words hold an intrigue for me.
Assembled into ideas of order-
A novel vicariously vivifies me!
And written in rhyme and meter,
A poem music can be-
And though not a poet and know it;
Writing is a pleasure for me!

## Mental Vacuum

There is a vacuum-
It sits there in my head-
I'd like to write a poem-
But nothing comes instead-
Gazing at my garden,
Perched at the farthest end-
Sat this yellow breasted warbler,
Then slowly in my mind-
It was then a surge of words kept flowing,
And a poem I did find!

## <u>Words of a Poem</u>

The words in a poem are special
You see,
For they spell out a meaning
To me-
They weave and they weave
Such colorful threads;
Into themes that vary
From happy to sad.
So the words in a poem are
Special you see-
They blend and reveal
Life's tapestry.

## <u>Inner Engine</u>

Early this January morn
My bed is nice and warm
It's then my inner engine refuses to perform
The mind a powerful ignition key
Starts priming ideas to me
And slowly as I leave this cozy nest
The engine revs
I leave this bed!

## A Game Of Scrabble

A kaleidoscope of words-
Sits up there in my mind-
Confusion sets in as I hope a
Script to find-
My senses on alert-
Start pushing words around-
They pick and choose and send
To me ideas that seem so
Sound-
And quickly as I jot them down,
Relief comes over me-
As the scrabble in my mind
Become poetry.

## Unwelcome Pest

I lead a wearisome life
Old age has arrived and stayed
Unwelcome this pesky guest
Controls mind matter and soul
Reviving days of old
When youth was daring and bold
So trudging along best we can
Let's tell this pest to scram!!

## Twenty Six Letters

Twenty six letters equipped me
For life-
They formed a helix that allowed
Me to write-
Vowels and consonants gather
In strength-
As ideas I write and write at
Length-
My thoughts though quiet
And self contained-
Unfold into a varied refrain-
Poems and essays and stories
Galore-
I tell you this alphabet-
Produces more and more!

## Snail Mail

This "Metamorphic Language"
Has me in a dither-
I know a snail is a snail and
Butterflies can fly-
But how can a snail become
My daily mail?

### The "Y-2K-Bug"

They are celebrating year 2000;
Techno, Bureau, and all "Crats".
Their minds were full of all
Calculations,
Pushing numbers from here to
That-
And so, on this year 2000,
How gleefully are they,
That successfully, under the
Rug was swept the
"Y-2-K Bug."

### Coins In A Pocket?!!!!

Money Market, Municipals, Ginnie Maes,
Etcetera,
Clatter like coins in a Stock Holders
Pocket.
Rates rise up and rates fall down,
As nervous investors blood pressure
Responds, rising and falling,
In tune with the Feds.
I'll gladly take Treasuries-
I'm telling you instead!!!!

DOT OSIKA

## Words

Just think what it would be
If no words had we,
The tree a tree wouldn't be,
For as you can see-
No word had we for a tree.
A phone would be useless
You see,
For a grunt or a moan
Wouldn't convey to thee
The image of a tree-
So, if no words had we,
I can tell thee,
That Mr. Gates would be
Really up a tree.

## Lost Space

I play the game fair and square-
Respect for others I do care-
While canvassing the parking lot-
I see for me a real good spot-
My right side blinker indicates,
My readiness to fill this space.
When suddenly a brash young Miss
Swerves boldly and deprives
Me of my parking place!

## "The Internet Stretch"

The boundaries of our nation -
Elastic once they seemed,
Stretched upward, downward,
Westward, and confident were
We,
United we stood stalwart,
From Atlantic to Pacific-
But now as I ponder,
This newest "Span-dex" stretch -
A thing called "The Internet"
Has insidiously set.
So the boundaries of our nation
Have once again stretched-
Into vast new areas on this
Thing called," The Internet".

## Due Diligence

I've done my due diligence,
Have you?
Tax exempt and taxable bonds
Do abound-
But minus due diligence-
The IRS, your money will abscond.

## Info Overload

Information overload,
Perplexes me profoundly-
For when I ponder about it,
What, when, and where is it?
Amazing numbers of retorts,
To me confusion exhibit!
So now the wireless and the
Wired, along with the written
Word-
Daily keep me guessing,
What's correct and not absurd?

## IRA THIS, IRA THAT?

IRA this, IRA that
How do I know where I'm at?
Stocks and Bonds and Mutual Funds,
Taunt and tease for a rainy day-
Graphs go up and graphs go down
Bouncing my IRA all around-
So how do I know where I'm at?
As virtual money is built on loose
Ground!

## <u>Cloning Thee</u>

The mysteries in each of us are
Many and complex-
Weaving daily patterns of demise
And success-
But now, just imagine,
If you were like me-
Forget it, a clone I, do not want to be!!

## <u>Cocooning</u>

I weave this thread of silk
About this place called home-
Intrusions of the phone by
Voices to me unknown-
Doorbell rung by folks whose
Wares I least care.
And ads galore sneak in -
Via radio, T.V. and mail-
So now this thread of silk
Increases length each day-
Cocooning me in a most
Relaxful way!

## "I'd Rather Be Me"

The wealthy rich impoverished
Within their daily rounds-
Customs that hold them within
Shackled bounds-
Designer clothes and jewelry,
Whose sparkle soon fades out-
Give rise to heavy boredom,
And a life just full of doubt-
But now as I am thinking,
I'd rather just be me-
And delve into a recipe, with
Hope and sometimes glee-
My daily rounds are simple,
No shackles bear me down-
But the makings of a recipe,
Can turn my world around!
As the cookies in the oven-
OOPS!  Are too brown!!!!

## Missing Links

Missing links of knowledge,
Present a handicap-
They remind me,
That I don't know where
I'm at!!

22

## How Is It Done?

My childhood fascination,
It sits deep inside-
About the plants that grow
Side by side-
Each time I view my garden
Whether veggies, flowers or
Shrubs;
There's something deep
Inside me-
That wonders how it's done!
The mystery of the carrot,
And the beauty of the rose,
Creates an awesome wonder
About how plants do grow-
And now while I am aging,
Slowly day by day-
I keep my childhood wonder,
Of, how it's all done?

## 20/20 Vision

That 20/20 vision,
I so dearly want to see -
It comes to me so lately -
When events by-pass me!

## **Good Gracious Grammar**

Grammar and syntax-such
Bug-a-Boo!
Dispel this myth-I'm telling you-
Construction of phrases and
Sentences too-
Can make or break whatever you
Do-
So piece together the rules of
Our language-
Then clarity and wisdom will
Shine on you!


## **"A Noggin Nugget"**

A nugget of knowledge found
In the quest-
Outstrips all gold mines found
In the west-
This nugget, its value has never
Been weighed,
But hear me, I tell you with
Each passing day,
The search for this nugget,
It will bring great dismay!

### "Awakening"

Spoken, written, or printed
From childhood to maturity-
I've blindly used the word-
Declensions, nouns, and
Pronouns, to say nothing
Of the verbs-
But as this day it dawns,
I've suddenly perceived-
Where would I be without
My friend, the word?
Spoken, written and printed,
This life giving word-
Has saved for society,
The best and absurd-
Oh! Where would we be
Without this talented
Word!!?

### "Quiet Relief"

The ads on the T.V., and radio galore,
Glaring in high pitch to sell us more!
Enough of this raucous-
I said to myself-
And trying it quiet for a spell-
I found I discovered a "New Self"

## Timeless Pleasure

As I rock with a sway-
The thought of time comes
Into play-
To and fro, with cushioned
Comfort-
The pendulum movement
Of my rocker,
Slowly lulls my daily pressure,
Leaving me a timeless pleasure-
But then the doorbell rings-
And back to time I dash again!

## Non Paid Entertainment

My ocular receptors of earthly
Events-
Perceive a range of videos,
By nature heaven sent-
This non paid entertainment
Exists for you and me-
If only time and vision are
Used wisely!!

26

## Are We Losing It?

Wired, wireless messages today,
Swifter than I am able to say.
Sent by people in a frenzied pace-
Their messages once spoken,
Evaporate.
Calm down! I say, and take to pen;
Write me a note, to be treasured
Then.
Let's prove to posterity
That we are lettered women
And men!

## "Form-idable Taxes"

So as I read lines a to g
I wonder who is taxed more
The IRS or me?
By April first I calculate
My last year's worth to
Keep on date!
Complex these forms of IRS,
Have made of me a mental mess.
So as I read lines a to g
I wonder who is taxed more ---
The IRS or me????

DOT OSIKA

## The Rides Of March 2001

March two thousand one,
Gave me a bumpy run-
The Dow and others did proclaim,
A nervously anxious refrain-
The lows outdid the highs today-
And so wiped out my previous gain!
This bumpy ride of March
This year,
Has built in me a Stock Market fear!!

## The Year Two Thousand and Two!

This two thousand and two year-
So full of news for us to bear-
Events of which you are aware-
Midst countries, people and
Global sections-
Let's call a meeting of minds, I say-
To solve this needless turmoil
At play-
An ounce of prevention would
Sweeten the brew-
The world would rotate in less
Of a stew!

## Heavenly Drones

Dear Lord, I ask you in these times
To open up my mind-
So I can better judge the things
Technology has sprung-
The impact of the Internet-
And also cellular phones-
Dear Lord, we ask for wisdom
Please-
To know these satellite drones!!!

## False Images

False images surround me,
Wherever I go-
How can I escape them-
I'd like to know-
Mass media diluted with ads
On the go!
Cartoons aplenty as violence
They show-
This onslaught of images, false
As they are-
Distort our youth's psychics
As they clamor for more!!!

## Carpe The Diem!

Carpe the diem, or if you don't-
The diem will carpe you-
And none will be done-
So seize it and use it, and
Then at dusk's end-
That diem fulfilled stops
Carping you then!!

## In Memory Of

This army of people-
I've known so long-
Where oh!  Where have they
Gone?
Through joys and sadness-
They marched along-
Equipped with their armors
Of love and toil-
They shouldered the battles
Of human travail-
As slowly they marched
To their ultimate end-
But now this lonely part
Of me,
Asks," Where this army of
Friends can be?"

## **Inner Orbits**

We carry our worlds within us-
Catching moments of encounter-
Amidst friends and foes-
Happy, irate or sad, up and
Down they go-
Weaving orbits -
I challenge you to know!


## **Seedlings Of Joy**

I awaken in the morning-
In a Ho Hum kind of way-
Not knowing that within me,
The seeds of joy and hope lay-
A routine kind of breakfast,
And chores of every day,
Keep moving my persona,
In a Ho Hum kind of way-
But then the sound of laughter,
And the chirping of the birds;
The voice of friendly people,
And the landscape in spring's
Rebirth-
Erupt the seeds within me-
Into seedlings of joy and mirth!

## Grammar-less Computer

The computer is here to stay
My friend,
So take heed this warning of
Current trends-
Graphics of icons, and acronyms plus-
You may wonder why I make such
A fuss-
Well, really the answer is simple
I say-
As you on your computer continue
To play-
Consuming what others have
Graphically to say-
Keep up the syntax and grammar
Skills-
To heck with the icons and
Acronyms plus-
Show me a name for namesake,
I say-
Not just an alphabet guessing game!!!

## A Free-Fall Flight

Virtual reality takes over in the
Night,
And then my mental journey goes
Into free-fall flight-
As dreams of "past gone" glories
Parachute me with delight-
And then my mental journey
Becomes a night-mare fright!

## Engine Repair

Did you ever rise up in the
Morning-
In a gloomy sort of way?
And the motor that's inside you,
Felt like gears worn away-
And inching to the kitchen,
The aroma of the day-
A good cup of java your
Motor regenerates.

## Me Myself Alone

I sit and write my poetry for
Me, myself, alone-
And when ideas I process into
Thoughts that tickle me-
I sit and have a chuckle
Over the poems with glee.

## Canvas Inspiration

My canvas introduces me-
To many intimacies.
There is this halfway hidden
Stone,
Peaking its head above the earth-
And very near a stump appears-
Wasting away with the years-
And a tree near by, thrusts its
Canopy into the sky-
And further down along the way-
Wild flowers scattered in colorful
Array-
Inspire within me -
To paint and paint away!

## "The Churning Wake"

The wake from my boat churns
Into the past-
As swiftly I steer my life into
Future fast-
Home is a safe port, where
Doldrums arise-
Give surge to an urge,
And with sails at full mast-
I captain my boat, leaving
The wake into the past.

## Don't Ask!

So you are nosing about my life
That's past-
I'll first tell you its events were
Not a huge blast!
But then again as I think on it,
How lucky I've to have last-
And now about my age you ask?
Well, telling my age, ages me fast-
So the date of my birth I keep
Secret steadfast-
And mentally grow younger as
The days pass and pass!

## Ill -Logic

I skirt around the issues-
And hem and haw away-
When the seams that hold
The logic,
Are swiftly ripped away-
The hem and haw within me-
No longer at play-
It's then I've decided-
Come what may!!!

## Flipping Along

The pages of my calendar,
Flip over month by month-
And before you know it-
A new year has begun-
And now in reminiscing,
On this first day of the year-
I'm glad that I've survived,
To flip another year.

## <u>Stop Counting!</u>

The season of our life-
I say should be-
A constant celebration,
Of springtime's exhilaration-
Forget the annual birthdays,
Reminding one of age-
Consider life one season-
No days and years to gauge-
As the onslaught of a number-
Is a stigma as we age-
But enjoy life as one season,
And become a happy sage!

## <u>The Race</u>

As I dawdled my life away
This thing called age came
And stayed-
But now my life is a faster
Pace-
As I hope that one of us -
Will win this race!

## Empathy

You haven't seen what feels
Inside-
Until you've had some hurt-
It's then that sympathy
Comes in and
Makes you so alert!

## The Stony Path

The stepping stones of life-
Lead into paths unknown-
Where life is met each day-
These paths begin and end
In most mysterious ways-
Giving us a wonder about
Each coming day!

## Know-Less

I write about the things I know,
And reading them-
Reveals to me, the more I write-
The less I know!

## A Grip On Grief

Grief and age have a grip
On me-
They squeeze, torment
And offer no glee-
But slowly each oncoming
Day,
A feeling of hope creeps
And allays-
The downside of grief but…
Not of old age!

## The Passing Months

The months they come one by one-
Looking back-
Where have they gone?
No sign of them have I to show,
Save for monthly bills I owe.
And yes there are these videos,
Of family, friends and even foes-
Of places and things
I cherish most-
That's where these past
Months repose!

## "My Race"

The clock it spins-
I hope to win,
I'm having a race with time-
The seconds, minutes and
Hours slip by-
And soon the day is gone-
But early on my list was done-
And confident that I had won-
Well "Hurry up Dot!"
A new day has begun!

## No Turn Off Click

I've trudged thru grief,
These many weeks-
The heart is heavy, the mind
Is slow-
As grief eats in and tears flow-
My mind in a happy past unfolds-
As brackets of a film of long ago-
But lo! This mental camera
Is not equipped with a
Turn off click!

## Best Of Our Human Race

Each day it comes and as it goes-
I hurry up my pace-
To slow me down would hinder most-
The marvels of this race-
So as each day it comes along-
I'm thankful for the grace-
To watch and see and utilize,
The best of our Human Race!

## Memory Bank

From dawn to dusk and even
At night-
From people and trees and
Landscape galore-
I gather and privately store-
Their antics, behavior and
Whatever more-
No hard discs have I in my head-
But only natural wonder
Instead-
And now as I walk sit or drive-
I carry this Memory Bank inside,
Increasing daily
My mental NET WORTH!

## Life's Game

We've played the game,
We think we've won-
Our life begins its downward
Run-
And as we think of days gone by-
Their highlights give us such a
Sigh!
But games begin and also end-
I'm glad I've played, and hope
I've won!

## "Denial"

I live in denial, they say to me.
But living this life, as cruel
Can be!
So when vicissitudes take aim
At me-
I seek other paths to set me free-
The hurts and pains are deep inside-
But denial for a while is soothing
For me-
Until finally comes reality!

## Millennial Eve

We're here to hold the past
Together-
For now and whatever!
For on this Millennial Eve;
The laser beams and fireworks,
Extend a glow heavenward-
Emitting sparks for hope next
Year-
Remembering all, that brought
Us here!

## Cliff Hanging Brink

I don't like the pressure of
Having to think-
Historical facts and numerical
Quizzes,
Carry me to cliff hanging edges-
But sunshine and flowers and
Home cooking odors-
Take over the pressure of
Hard thinking matters.

## <u>Anatomical Exposure</u>

Anatomy exposes me-
It names my bones and arteries-
Aortal, venous and ulnar seem-
So foreign and out of reach for me-
But deep inside there seems to be,
A sense of iove and poetry-
And bashful as I'm apt to be,
I cover up anatomy,
With a blanket of poetry.

## <u>Old Telephone Numbers</u>

My personal phone directory,
Has numbers of friends and
Family-
And as the year two thousand alit,
I start with sadness to edit,
So sad to scratch those dear to me-
They all were very close you see-
And now my thoughts as I reflect-
With them I had a warm connect-
The numbers gone- the memory
Is here-
Within me always very secure!

## My Self Taught Poetry

However trite, I bravely write,
My self taught poetry.
It comes and goes as thoughts
Occur, at times of reverie.

## Mini Bits

Mini bits of knowledge-
Pave roadways in my mind-
Opening vistas of wisdom-
As bright as all sunshine!

## Dot Says

1] The daily interactions,
Of life at work and play-
Leave one exhausted at
The end of day.
2] Poetical expression seeks
Words that spell it out-
Composed and put
Together-
It holds a lot of clout!

## My Mental Slate

Today I gave myself a lift-
A poem I did write-
The words they fell into place-
And cleared my mental slate-
In readiness for tomorrow's
Contemplate.

## Now And Then

I write a poem now and then-
But mostly when, the awesome
Sight of something there-
Compels the inner me-
To wordify the spirit that
So overtook me.

## Thinking Matters

I don't like the pressure of having to think.
Historic facts and numerical quizzes
Carry me to a cliff hanging brink.
But sunshine and flowers and
Cooking odors, relieve me so
Greatly of thinking matters!

## Verbals And Math

My verbals and math keep me
Daily in tow!
My check books don't balance-
I'm faced with a woe!
But honing my math I've
Recovered my dough-
The verbals I use are not
For show!

## Pattern 6793

Fashion patterns in the book-
Reveal to me a dressy look-
Laid out-cut and sewn-
Number 6793
Greatly disappointed me!

## "A Lemon"

There was a car from Missouri,
It spurted and raged like a fury-
When suddenly one day, its
Owner dismayed,
Junked the dang thing in a hurry.

## Inner Motive

There seems to be a motive-
To things I write about-
The thoughts that really
Move me, are enough to
Make me shout-
But shyness over
taking-
The pen wins out!

## Our Rosetta Stone

Joyful, Lamentful, whatever
In between-
The psalms that we've studied-
Show life's many themes-
From ancient, mediaeval and
Present day kings-
To humble and penitent
Human beings-
Their meaning translated
Into daily life-
Gives to us many insights.
And so I proclaim these psalms
To be,
The Rosetta Stone of life's
Mysteries.

## Household Chores

Household chores bore me-
I do them anyway-
Groaning, griping, cleaning-
And at the end of day-
I find that my boredom
Has neatly gone away!

## Dorothy's Secret

There is a little secret, it sits
There in the closet-
When blizzards snows deposit,
Disclosures of this secret-
May sound a bit banal-
But I am here to tell you,
It's Dorothy's cozy flannel!

## "A Sculptured Mind"

Setting words to music-
Gives lyricists a line-
Setting words to newsprint-
Keeps ever with the time-
But words set to poetry,
Reveals a sculptured mind!

DOT OSIKA

## "A Spinning Wheel"

A potter's wheel,
A clump of clay-
A mind, two hands,
They spin away-
The form evolves-
A big "HOORAY",
The potter sighs,
"A vase from clay!"

## Lend Me Your Ear

Lend me your ear and you will
Hear the things that are to me
So dear-
A child uninhibited at play with its
Toys-
A smile on a face illuminating joy-
The prose and poetry of inner
Deep reaches-
The music and paintings of all
The ages-
Indulging in these on a daily
Basis-
Has strengthened in me-
A hope for our race!

## Anxiety Engine

Anxiety keeps us going around-
When daily problems about us
Abound-
This engine runs like a spinning top,
Brakes on it do not stop.
But here it is this sunny day-
Perfect in every possible way.
"Anxiety leave me alone!", I say-
As I go out to enjoy this sun filled
Day.

## The Merry-Go-Round of Time

The merry-go-round of time-
Stops neither for you nor me-
No music or carnival horses,
Entertain as we go around-
So while on this circular race-
To enjoy the timely pace-
Snatch the ring of Gold-
Which holds mysteries untold-
And daily you will find-
The glories of the mind!

## Till We Meet Again

Each day they sustain us,
They left us and died.
We think and we wonder in
Grief and a sigh-
Yet imprinted upon us,
Their memory has life-
Giving us daily a better insight,
Of seeds of enrichment-
They planted deep within-
And now this life giving memory,
Flourishes till we meet again.

## My Mate Of Yesteryear

To and fro I go each day-
Reminded of a previous year-
When marriage made my life
Secure-
With children, husband and hope
Intact-
As daily life's challenges in us kept-
A fearless striving for better yet-
And then one day it is today-
I miss my mate of yesteryear-
As to and fro I go each day!

## Changing Shovels

Spring forgives the winter snows-
The blizzards with their forceful
Blows-
Forgiveness comes by increments-
When melting snows trade off their
Fury-
For springtime's budding glory-
And then tis time to change our
Mode, from snow to soil shovel.

## Gossamer Tints

March has finished its windy stride-
And now I watch the activity outside-
It is April you know!
So on with the show-
The past is the past with barren grays,
But here come the yellows, greens
And rusts-
Busily blending from morning to
Dusk-
Performance is subtle, but don't
Dismay-
For summer is coming one of these
Days!

## "A Mystery"

This speck confounds and
Amuses me-
For within it holds a mystery-
This speck will open up and
Grow-
And then unfold, the prettiest
Flower-a Marigold!

## A Scented Rose

I've taken for granted the
Scent of the rose;
But today, in the month of this
Blossoming June-
Events about me were out of
Tune-
But a walk in the garden
Restored my own bloom-
As I nestled my nose,
Into this petaled rose.
Inhaling a waft of a scent
So rare-
The events of the day were
No longer a care!

## My Moss Rose

My moss rose blooms in the sun-
I wish it would when day is done-
So, mid-day I meditate before
This colorful floral state-
The yellow and red into orange
Merge, petals so dainty and
Centers well set-
Imprint on my mind a joyful
Bloom-
Banishing thoughts of any gloom.

## My Miniature Rose

Buds of mini beauty-hold vast
Mystery-
As daily I attend them- with hope
And inner glee-
And a rapture engulfs me, when
Coral pink I see-
As if umbrella opened, it has
Solved this mystery.

## **Perennials**

Perennials keep growing,
Reviving northern hopes-
For summer's lush abundance-
On my perennial slopes.

## **Floral Glory**

They do not speak a word to me-
But look up so adoringly-
Aroma therapy they did invent-
Their aura seems heaven sent-
So as I walk this garden path,
Mid August blooms enjoy their
Sunshine bath-
Portulaca, Marigold, Zinnias their
Personalities unfold-
Magenta, yellow, rosy pink,
And on and on this story goes-
As various hues into petals show-
The blending glory of flowers
Aglow-
So as I walk along this path, no
Words need I to nourish
My soul.

## "Perennially"

My perennials annually
Surprise me-
When early spring arrives-
While clearing last falls
Leafings-
Beneath green hope thrives!

## A Blooming Surprise

The cutting I snipped in August
This year-
With hopes for a plant to give
Me some cheer-
Each day as routine beckoned
To me-
I watered and watched as this
Snip of a plant-
Began to erupt with leaves and
A stem-
This morn my hopes for cheer
Were fulfilled, as there on the
Window sill,
Looking at me, was a pretty
Pink bloom, a Geranium,
You see!

DOT OSIKA

## Spring Eruption

In spring my seeds erupted-
With inner hope of show-
The sun and soil provided-
The muscle for them to grow-
As rain and tender gardening,
Enhanced this future show-
And now my visual being,
Sees flowers all aglow.

## Spring!

So here it is the beginning
Of March-
Thoughts of defrosting snow
And ice-
Melt into spring's promises
Bright-
Enough of this dull wintry
Blight!
On with surges of growing life-
Bulbs, trees and seeds erupt
Into blooming delight.

## <u>Surprise!</u>

My seeds they slept their
Time away-
Until I planted them today-
And though a slow awakening,
Lo! And behold, some green I see-
And soon the mystery contained
Within,
Will blossom forth and,
Surprise me!

## <u>"Roads of March"</u>

The signs of spring are few and yet-
As March blows in with rains so wet-
My car encrusted with saline slush-
Will need a hose down with a brush-
The road ways still a saline white-
Are filled with potholes and what
A fright-
To drive around and in between-
Unpredictable as they are-
"Oops!" I've lost my hop scotch
Game-
As I blew a tire-
For shame, for shame!

DOT OSIKA

## "Hope"

I've never heard this before-
That hope from flowers springs
Forth-
And on this cold November morn-
My window sill with a flower is
Born.
I gaze and view this pretty bloom-
So fragile pink, yet full of life-
Inspiring me to meet winters
Strife-
The winds they come, the winds
They go, but bravely pink
My flower glows-
And so each day with loving care-
I tell you HOPE for spring is there!

## "The Rain"

With grateful hearts, we
Greet thee rain-
For dryness was our
Withering refrain-
We hoped, we looked,
We searched in vain,
Until this day, down came
The RAIN!

## Jack Minus A Ladder

Stalwart my pole beans stand
Upright-
Reaching limits beyond my height-
And now as I climb the rungs of my
Ladder-
It comes as a wonder, how
Jack and the Bean Stalk
Climbed high into yonder!
But steady am I on the rungs
as I climb, and glad that I'm
DOT and not Jack in a bind!!!!

## April's Merge Into May

The rain is falling, like dew drops
From heaven-
All foliage responds with unfolding
Pleasure-
The weather man takes note of
This rainfall measure-
Relief is in sight, from this drought
Laden plight-
As April merges into May's
Floribunda might!

## Moss Rose Mystery

Fascia, magenta, cherry red,
Pink-
Orange, bright yellow and shades
In-between-
My Moss Rose unfolds its palette
To me-
As I gaze in wonder,
"How can such beauty be?"
And then a calm feeling
Permeates me-
As I stand near these flowers
Of awesome mystery!

## The Arid Muse

My well is dry, no thoughts
Arrive-to glorify this day-
What can I do to stimulate
This arid muse within?
T'is early spring and look!
My potted seeds have sprung!
These mini bursts of energy,
Have greatly me revived!
And now the dormant muse
Within, has brightly come
To life!

## A Springtime Spring

What do you know?
Spring has sprung!
Life giving sap is on the run-
Giving each tree, seed and bulb-
Energy for a spectacular show!
Branches inert these past
Winter months-
Awaken and don their best
Spring duds-
Dressed in the gentlest, daintiest
Hues-
Their garments most stylish,
Their aromas divine-
What's not to love?
"This great Springtime!"

## "Zucchini"

Popping thru microbial soil,
Well tended last month,
With gardeners toil-
This gentlest sprout, I
Vision to be, the greenest,
Most succulent, you
Guessed it-Zucchini!

## My Silent Partner

I have this silent partner
It speaks volumes to me
And if you wonder
How can this be?
It opens up my world
To people, places, and events
And quietly my evenings are well spent
As comfortably at home
The outside world I roam
While vicariously I read
This voluminous tome!

## Fall

I've "Beddy-byed" my garden,
As Fall descends on me-
And flowers on dried-out
branches, droop down their
Worn-out heads-
The static frozen images of
Trees and lawns and shrubs,
Give rise to a stalwart promise-
Of a bountiful harvest to come!

## **Fall's Chemistry**

Mid September and change
Prevails-
Chemistry of nature is fast
At work-
These micro-reactions in
Canopied trees-
Affect the cells of all the leaves-
The symphonium of labor
Consistent each Fall,
Brings landscape beauty,
For one and all!

## **"Melting Reflections"**

There's not much I can tell you
On this bright October day-
Except that birds are feeding,
As they migrate on their way-
The trees are sending signals,
With their colors on display-
That soon it's time to harvest,
The thoughts of summer' day-
And use these warm reflections,
To melt winter's icy sway!

## Dutiful Leaf

I've done my duty fair and
Square-
By hanging upright in the air-
Nor wind, nor rain could get
Me down-
For duty kept me branch-
bound-
But now that summer has
Met its end-
It's time that I should float
To earth-
And give next springtime's
Leaves their birth.

## Timely Glory

The sunny hours of sundials-
Are in tune with my Moss Rose-
The one it counts the hours-
The other opening its flowers-
Performs a colorful show-
But time erodes the beauty
Of my Moss Rose-
As petals surrender their
Glory to next year's growth.

## "My Daughter's Veggie Garden"

My daughter's veggie garden,
Produces mysteries-
As unknown eruptions raise
Heads randomly-
These complex riddles are fun
To watch and see-
When at the end of summer,
Within this old pine tree-
Hang three plump pumpkins-
Fleshly big and round-
Ending this saga, as they are
Kitchen bound!

## Nature's Code

Amazing shapes in nature grow-
From sunflowers to trees and
Veggies we know-
No matter the seed, the plant
Will emerge-
Obeying faithfully it's built in
Code-
But, tell me, I ask, "Can a lab with
A flask, stealing the patent of
Nature's past, make seeds
And bulbs for us at last!"

## Leaves Of Earth

This windy late October day-
My backyard trees shed their
Colorful array-
One by one these chips of color,
Sail playfully mid air to earth-
They've sheltered us from
Summer's heat-
And gave us air so good to
Breathe-
And now that fall has beckoned
Them-
Obediently they fall to earth-
And as we rake and rake away-
Let's treasure the compost,
These leaves have made!

## Toiling Soil

My toiling soil works hard
For me-
Its microbes making chemistry-
While plants thrive there,
Symbiotically,
I wait for veggies with a glee!

## "A Basket Case"

As I weave my thoughts about
Them-
Looking at these baskets-
I look and wonder on them-
Raw materials of nature-
The ups and downs and
All around, give nimble fingers
A challenge-
As reeds and ropes and shaved
Woods, are skillfully crafted-
It's then my weaving thoughts
Perceive the beauty of
These baskets.

## A Censored View

Images are dimmed this winter
Morn-
No crispness, no sparkle, no
Shining sun-
And as yet as we look and
Determine the view-
The woods and the fields in
A peaceful mood-
Are censoring their secrets
With fog today.

## Autumnal Mystery

Nature's master paint brush-
Wields a powerful stroke-
Creating subtle changes-
That end into a glow-
The windows of my great room
Provide this wondrous show,
Of tints and shades of colors,
Along the field below-
My elevated vista brings canopies
To me, of greens and reds and
Oranges-
Found nowhere else you see-
For nature holds her patents so
Very secretly-
As artists try so vainly to solve
This autumnal mystery.

## Winter's Jewels

Sleet sleeting, branches icing-
Sleet stopping, sun shining-
Branches twinkling, lights
Aglow-
Diamonds sparkling,
Trees bejeweled in a
Crystalline show!

## Last Blooms Of Fall

Well, it's the first of October,
September was mild-
I stand in my garden, imprinting
In mind-
The summer's production of
Flowers sublime-
The moss rose and marigold,
Alyssum too-
Burst out into a colorful spree-
Dainty and pretty as if just
For me-
Wistful am I of approaching
Frost-
These blooms in my memory
Will not be lost!

## Negatives In The Snow

The twigs and trunks and branches-
Outlined in morning's snow-
Cast a negative of whatever
Is below-
Developing films in dark rooms,
Technology intense-
Can't match the awesome image,
Of negatives in the snow!

DOT OSIKA

## **The Buck Stops For Me**

The stand of trees at the brink
Of my lot-
Have sheltered me from past
Summer, so hot-
Their canopy swept this
Autumn with winds-
Barren they stand, extending
My view to this pasture land-
Fall is upon me, my view
Opens up-
And this morning guess what?
There, mid-meadow stood,
A six pointed Buck!!!

## **Keeping Alive**

The cleansing cover of winter's snow-
Trees their random shadows throw-
Foot prints, ,mysterious, I'd like to
Know; a rabbit, a squirrel, or a fox
On the prowl?
These clues !eave a wonder-
What animals thrive-
Out there in winter, keeping
Alive!

## A Bushy Tail

I thought I'd written all there
Is, about the fallen snow-
But then one day, beyond the
Field I gazed-and WHOOO!!!!
This brown is orange creeping
Creature, stealthily crept
His way-
This form had stopped and
Suddenly,
It spiraled up and curled
Around and downward
Crashed the snow-
It surfaced quickly and with
A lick, devoured its prey-
And very foxily stole away,

## A Springless Walk

T'is the week after Christmas-
And at home I am today-
As yesterday I walked the Mall-
And people I did see-
Impassively they trudged along-
The old amidst the young-
And as they moved so aimlessly,
I thought their spring had sprung!

## **Fraternal Leaves**

The leaves of my oak, fraternal
Are they-
Budding in spring, greening in
Summer-
And now on this mid November's
Day-
The wind stirred them all and
said; "T'is time for oak leaves to fall!"
And so these brethren garbed in
Russets and tans,-
Message received and together
They fell!

## **Sparkles**

Early morning sparkles,
Brighten up the snow-
Catching rays of sunshine,
Emitting such a glow-
Gems of carat beauty,
Perform a winter show-
And as the day is ending,
Where did this beauty go?

## Crisp White Snow

On this Sunday morning, when
The snow is crisp and clean-
I view the distant pasture, and
What do you think?
While watching this serenity,
In distance I behold-
A black line writing a message
In the snow-
You'd think it was an E-mail
Visible to me-
But no t'was a black crow,
Swooping down to feed.


## The Lonely Last Leaf Of Winter

The last leaf of winter, waves clinging
To the branch-
Reminding me of glory, this leaf once
Had-
The vibrant green aliveness, endured
The summer past-
In rain and sunshine showers, this
Leaf held steadfast-
And now as spring approaches,
This leaf must let go at last!

## A Sandpaper Thrust

Branches and twigs lit up with
A glow-
Tree trunks all covered with ice
And snow-
As snuggly at home I watch this
Show-
But further than that I know I
Must leave this beauteous scene-
And pursue the roads with their
Perilous gleam-
Thankfully behind the sandpaper
Thrust,
Of dutiful road crews, in their
Ice blasting trucks!!!!

## A Suet Bite

The frosted limbs of barren
Trees-
Reveal to me a winter's freeze-
As birds of bush with winged
Flight-
With eager beaks, our suet bite!

## Stalactiting

The prism of the icicles-
Reflect the sunny rays-
Stalactiting abundant arrays-
These long and pointed beauties-
Their prime on frigid days-
Begin their sorrowful droppings,
On warm spring days-

## "A Non-Snow Blower Event"

The rhythm of time keeps me going
Around, as Fall creeps into Winter-
The fallen raked leaves hibernate
In the ground-
And perennials promise their
Springtime rebound-
But here I remain, pondering
Winter's refrain-
Snow Blow! Snow Blow!
And away I go pushing drifts of
Snow-
In rhythm with time and suddenly,
WHOA!!!
My motor won't go-
And I'm out of tune with time!

## Slippery Slopes

Slippery, steep ski slopes, provide
Life with a thrilling ride-
The endless trails we rate, for
Difficulties we take-
Seem varied and confusing-
But arriving at the base-
We think life is quite a race!

## Birding

The act of birding is so startling,
In bushes trees and fields-
Footsteps gentle as can be,
Suddenly erupt a feathered
Spree-
The cardinal cloaked in brilliant
Red-
His mate, not far, but just ahead-
The Chick-A-Dees, black hats in
Place, and Blue Jays also enter
The race-
And here I stand in bewildered
Wonder-
As feathers fly into Nature's
Yonder.

## Fall Too

This is a day for poetry and
Nature is all about-
Busily doing her earth work;
In a manner worth a shout!
The birds are at my feeder,
The leaves have blanketed
The lawn-
The trees are shorn of cover,
And Fall has just begun!


## A Heave And A Ho!

These dainty mini flakes of
White, keep falling out there,
Day and night-
Clothing trees and all in sight-
And as I look and peer outside-
My mind gives rise to a southern
Flight!
But thoughts are thoughts and
Deeds are deeds-
So shovel in hand, I proceed-
With a Heave and a big HO!
I shovel the snow.

DOT OSIKA

## Flickering Flight

There's flickering life, in my
Evergreen tree.
Look quickly, it's there-
It's a Chick-A-Dee!

## The Trade Mark

This black capped lively little
Bird-
As sprite as he could be,
Alit onto my feeder and pecked
So heartily-
He whisked away so quickly,
But I know him a Chick-A-Dee
To be.
This precious little creature, it
Flies so artfully-
Defying aeronautics and
Performs each day for me-
His feathered garb is stylish-
I never tire to see-
His charming little black cap-
A trade mark for every
Chick-a-dee!

## Secret Journey

I wonder where from?
Their journey a secret-
Their paths well flown,
Arriving in March, into
New York's wet snow-
Welcome wee birds, from
I don't know where-
And glad you made it-
From way out there!

## Bird Watch

A dreary February morning,
As I viewed my seed-filled
Feeder,
A ball of fluffed gray feathers-
Awoke my winter "druthers"-
I raced to my major reference,
"The Perching Bird Guide Book"-
Not sparrow, nor titmouse
Was he-
This ball of fluffed gray feathers-
But turning the page with glee-
I found him a Junco to be!

## Sky Writing

A cloud of geese darkened
The sky-
Their rotorized wings,
Motored them high-
With energy blest, they
Continued to fly-
Writing goose messages
In the sky!

## Zesty Pecks

They don't take much, a couple
Of pecks-
And off they fly with so much
Zest!
So, now I wonder about these seeds-
How nourishing they are to feed
These birds of flight, with so much
Might!
And further more I cogitate-
The beauties of my feathered friends-
Their beaks, their tails, and plumage all-
Each species special from spring to fall-
Binoculars, I have to view them all!

## Shades Of Winter Brown

T'is early Sunday morning-
The fields are white with snow-
In various depressions, are
Signs of last year's growth-
This one time multi-greenery
Has aged to shades of brown-
Holding seeds life giving-
That our winter birds have found.

## A Cardinal View

T'is March and weary from
Winter's gloom-
But, Lo! and Behold!
What do I see?
With a flash of delight, on the
Last of winter's snow-
There sits this Red Cardinal,
With brightness aglow-
The weariness of winter
Melts slowly away-
By the sight of this creature,
With its gorgeous array!

## Mental Space

The view thru my window,
Gives sunny delight-
As I watch Blue Jays and Cardinals
In their energy flights-
Now, the meditative process
Requires a quiet place-
Away from the hurly burly
Of our over powered pace-
And so I will settle for my own
Mental space!

## A Morning Treat

I've had my treat for the
Morning-
A Cardinal came to feed-
Now, given the February
Backdrop, of tans and grays
And blacks-
How striking to my psyche,
To see this brilliant red-
A bright spot midst this
Drabness,
Is a treat that I've just had!

## The Little Robin

A Little Robin was hatched today-
His nest a home for him to stay-
But as all fledglings seem to know,
There is a time for them to go-
And so it came that awesome day,
When he bewildered flew away.

## Barren Trees

The frosted limbs of barren
Trees-
Reveal to me a winter's freeze-
As birds of bush with winged
Flight-
With eager beaks, our suet bite!

## The Wingless Kite

Soaring high-encircling the
Sky-
Early on a morn-
The sparrow hawk, in its
Stringless flight-
Out did my wingless kite.

## My Favorite?

If you asked me for my favorite,
I just couldn't say-
The Chick-a-Dee so flighty-
Brings me much glee-
The adornment of the Cardinal,
An eye catcher for me-
And then comes the Blue Jay-
Authority in full sway-
Feathered in blues from purplish
To gray-
And then the little Junco, on
Ground feeds he-
Slips under my feeder for
Me to see.
And as for my favorite-
I can only say-my vote goes
To the feathered kingdom-
To birds of all sway!

## A Pecking Gourmet

A bunch of varied birds one day-
Enjoyed our pecking seed gourmet-
The Dees, and Finches with
Nut Hatches,
Energetically ate big batches!

## Hawk Eye

The Hawk in the tree, sits
Anxious to see his prey of
The day-
And then ferocious is he,
Swooping to earth-
Precise to the spot-
Equipped with a vision of
A Bull's Eye Shot!

## "Window"

The view thru my window gives
Sunny delight-
Thoughts in my mind that rise
Higher than kites-
Blue Jays and Cardinals in energy
Flights-
Open my vistas to autumnal
Sights-
Canopied trees disrobe their
Leaves and stalwartly wait for
Winter's big breeze-
The view thru my window
Refreshes my mind-
As daily a new mystery unwinds!

DOT OSIKA

## A Chirping Refrain

My back bedroom window
Overlooks a field-
And each morning, the bush birds
Start their day-
The airwaves of their chirping-
Greet me with a message my way-
Their bird talk is chirping-
"Dot, time to start your day!"

## Consumer Rage

Up and down the aisles I roam-
in search of next weeks meals-
Budget fixed to meet my needs-
Confusion sets right in-
Five pounds of rice would be nice-
But where oh! Where is the
Unit price?
So on and on I go-
Till loaded down with next weeks
Meals.
You've guessed it -
My budget I did blow!

## **The Red Polls**

The red polls are back-
I wonder from where?
Their journey a secret,
Their course they well know-
Arriving in March, into
New York's wet snow-
Welcome! Wee birds from
I don't know where-
And glad you made it
From way out there!

## **Air Alert!**

The air I breathe I cannot see-
To me that is a mystery-
Unseen this gift of life sustains
our every day existence-
It asks no payment for its work-
And totally surrounds us-
And now it's time to mind,
Oh, "TECHNO MAN",
The preservation of this gift of
Respiration!

## "A Free Vacation"

Flocks of birds flying in
Peppered formations-
Dotting the sky with myriad
Migrations-
Southerly winging their
Warm expectations,
Find for themselves
A free vacation.

## A True Fisherman!

There is this young fellow named Greg-
To go fishing with you he would beg-
Hook, line, and sinker along with bait-
Are enough to send Greg into a
Serious fishing state!
A cast of the line into water sublime-
Raises hopes for the catch of the day-
Lo! And Behold! At the bend of the pole,
Our Greg pulls up and,
"What do you know?"
The battle begins - Who will win?
Greg or what's at the end of the line?
Well, Greg, true fisherman that he is,
Will tell you this -
"It sure was a big one that got away!!!"

### Rata-tat-tat!

There was a curiosity that
Held me in its grip-
As I looked about our garden-
My eardrums almost split!
For in the tree trimmed distance-
On a barren limb of oak-
Clung a woody wood pecker-
Rata-tatting his hammering strokes!

### My Kitchen Friends

I have many kitchen friends,
And actions they do do!
They neither speak nor criticize
My culinary art-
But when those chocolate chips
Are done-
My timer friend alerts and buzzing
Sends me to the oven-
Avoiding cookies burnt-
My list of kitchen buddies grows
More mundane each day-
As pot holders, peelers, and
Knifers,
Continue their friendly sway!

## Nature's Camouflage

The barren branched trees of
Winter-
Show bird plumage so varied to me-
But when buds of spring's arrival,
Burst into a coverage of green-
My lenses focused intently, on
Bushes and branches to see-
The birds that now so cleverly,
Know how to evade me.

## Micro-Wave Meal

Did you ever notice?
When the Micro-Wave is on-
The annoyance of the beeper
Alerting you to come-
Upon investigation- a survey
Of the dish-
You poke and stir and wonder?
"Is this meal really done?"
So full of hopeful wishing-
The Micro-Clock reset-
Diverted to the doorbell-
A visit with your guest-
You better know it-
The Micro-Meal's a mess!

## Nature's Seed Harvest

Birds on my backyard feeder-
Intrigue me day by day-
Pecking seeds of vigor-
And quickly fly away-
Swift as dreams and visions,
Flying to their nests-
Nourished by the mystery,
Of Nature's seed harvest.

## A Fallen Cake

Steaming, roasting, frying-
The chemistries in my kitchen-
Work mysteries each day-
Formulas for cooking are recipes
They say-
But here in my kitchen, I'm always
In dismay-
As testing, tasting, wondering,
How these chemistries will come
Into play-
While the cake is in the oven-
The timer chimes away-
I find the Baking Powder,
I did forget to blend!

## Streaks Of White

Bands of winter's forest-
Carpeted in white-
Careless drapes of shadows-
Twixt broken streaks of light-
Reveal cavorting pleasure-
of fawn and deer delight.

## Leaping Deer

Balleting across the field of
Snow-
A herd of deer put on a show-
Arching leaps of dancing
Splendor-
Moved the troupe to fields
Down yonder.

## Out Of Sight

I respect the Chick-A-Dee,
Its fast and furious flight-
Directed at the feeder,
It takes a mini bite!
And off into the bushes,
I lose it out of sight.

## "Wordless"

Alone with my thoughts,
At the bay window-
An open field, wordless, and still
Speaks of images, what a thrill!
As Chick-A-Dees, Blue Jays and
Black Birds emerge-
Chirping and cawing-
Who needs words!

## Fourth Floor Ocean-Front

My fourth floor ocean-front
Offers a vast sense of perspective-
The endless horizontal skyline-
Move forward to a surf of
Beating fury-
Washing the sandy beaches-
With laces of foaming beauty-
Humans are roaming the beaches-
Each in varying ability-
Some in aerobic swiftness-
Some in age worn limits-
Others in child-like gambit-
Enjoying nature's provisions.

## "Patented Flights"

The feathery flights of birds,
Create a wonderment of awe-
As aeronautically they fly
Without flaw-
So engineers of flight-
Take stock of creatures,
As airily they move with,
Nature's patented secrets!

## Italian Deli

The whims of my Belly-enjoyed
The local Deli-
The gratings of Romano, Fennel,
and Parmesano-
Blend into Italiano!
As the whims of my Belly-enjoy
The local deli-
And when it comes to sausage-
The linkage goes to Rome-
A sausage pepper sandwich-
Is enough to send you home!

## "A Perfect Pitch"

The perfect pitch of Phoebes-
Flies through the air so sweetly-
Mid April's barren branches-
Bursting with May's secrets-
Tarmacs for air borne Masters-
Of nesting and flight ability-
Look up! Around! Listen!
The perfect pitch of,
"Phoebe, Phoebe"

## Little Friends

My little friends on this snow covered
Day-
Perch brotherly as they peck away-
On the gourmet selection of seeds on
Display-
Their "Thank You" to me is enough
You see-
As I gaze on their antics of
Bird energy!

## What Is It?

It suddenly came to me,
What is this thing I cannot see?
The hour glass sand it can hold,
but lose whatever it unfolds-
Clocks and watches measure it-
and to its march we all submit-
But here I am a baffled me-
Asking still: "What's aging me?"

## "High Tide"

A piece of drift wood, dear to me-
Recalling scenes along the beach-
The raucous sea gulls-on alert-
Outwit each other for all their
Worth-
And as I gaze on raging surf-
The stoic pelicans emerge-
Their line of flight precision
Perfect-
Skimming bravely over surf-
And as I stroll in awesome
Wonder-
The tide rolls in and I dash out!!

## The Din Din Odyssey

Rice Cider, Balsamic and many
More-
An odyssey into a store of galore-
Italo, Mex, Jewish and more-
Distractions abound with each
Label I view-
Italo sounds good;
The Jewish blintz, a hit of the day-
Wandering the aisles of ethnic
Display-
Rice Cider, Balsamic and Vinegars
More-
Confusion sets in, at a rapid pace-
And I head for the frozen food
Refrigerator case-
And Lo! This odyssey comes to
An end-
As I pull out, you guessed it-
The ready made "Din Din".

## Verse Prose

Prose is prose,
Verse is verse,
I like one better,
The other one verse!!!

DOT OSIKA

## Onion Peeler

If you can peel an onion,
And not give eyes a cry-
If you can fry an onion,
And eat it with a sigh!
Then the gourmet that's
Within you-
Gets this great big "HOORAH."

## House Wifely Courage

The tempus it fugits-
I know not where-
But questions unanswered,
Just give me more dare-
So given this timely quandary-
I'll proceed to do my laundry!

## My Meniscus Eye

And when it comes to measuring-
My goodness Me, Oh, My!
Its then my cup runneth over,
With highly accurate pride-
As the cake in the oven,
Obeys my Meniscus Eye!

## Bashful Me

I do my best cooking, while
No one is looking-
This is true of whatever I do-
My accomplishments are
Private-
No scrutiny can I bear-
For shyness overcomes me-
With the slightest critique
They dare.

## Neighbor Across The Street

I have this neighbor across the street-
She's someone you would like to meet-
Her home made pizza and roasted
Peppers-
Are a few of her kitchen pleasures-
If you should ever choose to meet-
This lady across the street-
Prepare yourself for lots and lots
Of tasty treats.

## A Nervous Ride

Our nation's swift highways-
Give one a nervous ride-
As fast and furious drivers,
Leave good manners far aside-
These super speeded roadways,
Allow me to make haste-
But don't you think that-
Ultimately it's a lot of waste!

## The Breakers

The breakers are breaking the
Silence around-
As thunderous waves come
Crashing aground-
Undaunted and graceful,
The pelicans fly-
Mindless of furies that
Under them lie-
OH! That we should mimic-
The piloting beauty of
Nature's might!

## Tail Gating

How gentle are you feeling,
In traffic on your way-
When cars come careening-
In various swings and sways-
How gentle are you feeling-
When speed laws you obey-
And someone shouts behind
You, "Get out of my way!!!!"

## Waves

Swishing, swashing, booming-
Waters from the sea-
Beachward, briny journey-
Ends smashingly!

## Car From Missouri

There was a car from Missouri-
It spurted and raged like a fury-
When suddenly one day,
Its owner dismayed-
Junked the "DANG" thing in a hurry!

## **Lost Pencil**

Oh, if I could find my pencil-
How verbosely I would write-
Of the multilayered roadways,
Entwined about the earth-
My pencil would continue to
Elaborate in full-
About the high and by-ways,
And their land consuming skill-
The linear encroachment winds
a merciless track-
Replacing life green areas-
With a deadly look of black-
My stylus would gain recognition,
As it sallied forth admonition-
To men who fallibly create-
While we revolve, rotate, and
Stagnate-
OH!  If I could find my pencil!!!

## **Where Is The Horizon?**

There is no horizon on the sea-
The cloudy mist reveals to me-
Swashes of mega waves galore-
Rushing furiously ashore!

## Ripe Old Age

Old age has got me-and
He won't let go-
He grips me in my walking,
And running is no show-
Old age may ripen cheese-
But please, Mr.------
"Have mercy on me!!"

## Air Noise

My home a steady comfort to me,
Has been invaded by an enemy-
The wired and wireless with a flick
Of the switch-
Rattle my eardrums, with a
Raucous pitch-
The ads and promotions on
Airwaves galore-
Test patience, endurance
Evermore!
Then somewhere within this
Noisy clamor,
I must hurry to get today's
Weather!

## Worryful Life

I lead a worryful life-
Oh! Crossing the street is a
Fright!
Cars to the left-cars to the
Right-
Make crossing the street,
A pedestrian plight-
Oh! I lead such a worryful
life!

## "Money Gears"

I own a money factory-
Its gears are Stocks and Bonds-
And as each day the values sway-
These gears churn round and
Round-
My factory issues forth reports-
That profoundly affect my mind-
But then as I reflect on life -
And know the ups and downs-
It's then I say "Stay calm and
Watch these gears turn round
And round."

## A Journey To The Beach

Come with me on a journey, to
The booming, surfing beach-
Where onward falling waters,
Merge rhythmically-
While Seagulls and Pipers-
Scavenge food for them to eat-
Come with me on this journey-
Which meets SOUL with the sea!

## Dot's Advice

Do I have an opinion?
Bet your boots I do!
Politics, economics, and home
Repair-
Add to it gardening, cooking, and
Cutting my hair!
Opinions I give without any charge-
But the price you will pay for my
Free advice-
Will put weeds in the garden-
Over cooked rice-
An overdrawn bank book-
And a coif with a look-
You wished not to have!!!

## Pelican Flight

The air along the ocean is so
Fresh and deep to breathe-
To walk the sandy shores-
Brings joy beyond belief-
The aero-flight of Pelicans,
In measured pace on high-
Sends calm to the senses-
While walking with a sigh!

## Poetic Challenge

Poetry, oh, poetry, how you
Challenge me-
I see the waves on oceans
Shores and Pelicans galore-
But put to words this seascape
Show-
Escapes me evermore!

## Foamy Froth

The frothy foamy ocean rises
Out of the deep-
Bringing thrusts of energy
For you and me to see!

## Sheller's Delights

Azure blue horizon, meeting
Outer skies-
Sending forth white caps,
Merging into surf-
Wetting sandy beaches,
Revealing sheller's delights-
Cockle shells, scallops, and
Shark's teeth with ancient bite-
Azure blue horizon,
What a sheer delight!

## Sand Prints

The rain swept sand on beaches
End-
Was smooth and ready for
Prints of man-
But look! And see I notice
There-
Tail tracks scratched and
Then seaward bound-
I know not where-
The turtle marked its print
In sand!

DOT OSIKA

## Sculptured Beauties

Slowly sauntering on the beach-
The tide is out, the shells are in-
I gather them with love within.
These sculptured beauties,
Reveal to me-
The sandblast effort of the sea!

## Auto Praise

I am a senior citizen
With car memories of long ago
Autos of past eras were no great show!
And now the sands of time
Have ushered in on stage
Performing cars:  currently the rage!
To engineers I say, "Hooray!  Hooray!"
For setting on stage
The cars that perform this play
With beauty, comfort and ease
So now, as I drive
My new ford focus
I am so very pleased!

## Sandpiper Spirit

Sandpiper spirit captured me-
As I walked along the edge of
The sea-
Their flittering, scampering
Energy-
Hastened my gait as they nipped
At the sea-
Sandpiper spirit captured me-
As I marveled at the mysteries
About me!

## My Wireless Wonder

My computer and I are at odds today-
As"User Friendly" refuses to obey-
Booting doesn't have a kick-
It's then I search the "How To Book!"
With hopes to find the start up trick!
My mouse, as anxious as mice can be,
Sits there smirking at me-
While reading, hoping almost
Pleading-
I notice my wireless wonder
Was unplugged!!!

DOT OSIKA

## Solace

Walking the beaches of sand-
Take over the thoughts of man-
The pounding surf, the call of the
Gulls-
Erasures of mental activity-
Introduce hypnotic tranquility-

## Sandy Tarmac

The azure reflecting sea,
Mirrors an image of tranquility-
Sea gulls soaring in the sky-
Gracefully pilot their weightless
Flight-
While ocean's ebbing tidal flow-
Widens the sandy tarmac below!

## EARLY MORNING POETRY

Early morning poetry resolves my get up and go.
I sit and write of things to do,
with great poetic verve.
But musing on this wake up call-
Time came and went and then,
Dot's morning is all spent.

## Westward From The Sea

Wow! What huge and churning waves-
Keep booming westward from the sea-
They fiercely whitewash rows of
Beaches-
Sculpturing shells into varied beauty-
Once these booming waves of nature-
Calm their beachward onslaught-
Oh! What joy to roam those sands,
Combing out their treasures!

## Mental Menu

My thoughts are in sink with the
Weather today-
Grey clouds and dampness make
It difficult to think-
My mental capacity spurred on
To the brink-
It's then that necessity of food
And drink-
Replace the gloom of weather
Today-
As I dash to the kitchen,
My menu at hand-
It's then that my mind is in
Full command!

DOT OSIKA

## My Genetic Clock

My genetic clock ticks me off-
Each day I look at me and say-
"Oh, why am I built this way?"
But then as I looked around-
Acceptance slowly I did find-
And as this genetic clock ticks on-
I'm grateful for my body and
Mind!

## A Silent Language

There is a silent language-
It permeates the air-
No lexicon is needed to decipher
The message so pure-
The purple colored pansies,
With yellow hallowed heads-
Rise up their pretty faces,
To me and said-
"Hello! And glad to see you."
And then I answer back-
"Your silence is a language,
I comprehend at last!"

## Non-Stop Age

Tick tock, tick tock-
Advancing my age non-stop-
This measured master of
Timely pace-
Has me running a ragged race-
Yesterday spent-today is here-
The tick of the clock-
Looks to another year!

## Word Challenge

I stammer and I studder-
As an idea comes into my
Head-
I love the subject dearly-
My eyes and ears tell me!
But creating a poem essay,
Is a word challenge you see!
So I stammer and I studder,
As I stumble into words-
That rarely gives true feeling,
In my poem essay verse!

## My Word Tree

My word tree is precious to me-
Ever bearing fruits that I need-
Branches outstretched-
Growing each day-
Dangle words that I put into play-
Poems, essays, and so much more-
OH!  Where would I be without
This tree?

## Wake Up Call

Eras of history have passed us by-
Events of glories and tragedies
Silently lie-
Waiting for scholars to open their
Books of archival voices-
Urgent to tell," Repeat not our
Errors, or you will burn in Hell."

## End of Day

The daily inter-actions
Of life at work and play-
Leave one exhausted
At the end of day.

## **Inner Compass**

Uncharted was my road of life-
And thus I traveled, no atlas to
Guide my stumbling stride-
"Don't stop - but forge ahead!"
This road it winds in bumpy ways-
And now that I am old and gray-
The stumbles I've had along
The way-
Have charted my road of life
Today!

## **Zee Strokes At Night**

Clap clap clap, boom zoom boom-
Zee strokes of bright, white light-
Streak the sky this night-
The fireworks on display-
The winds they blow and blow-
Driving this pyretic show-
And here am I, in awe and
Awful fright-
As the boom and zoom groans
Noisily into the night-
Giving me hope for a quiet,
Sun filled day!

DOT OSIKA

## The Autumn of Life

Fall has finally fallen on us.
Out door faucets and hoses drained.
Braced against winter's severe strain!
And leaves dressed in greenery all
Summer long.
Disrobe and reveal their bright inner self.
The woodland aglow at this time
Of year.
Then on signal from Nature's request.
Obediently these leaves
Come to Earth for a rest.
Now the season of fall upon us
The greenery of life slowly
Changes it hue.
And Dear ones we love
Obey the call
As fond memories we have
And recall and recall!

## The Flying Minute

Catch the minute, it's flying away-
Where it goes-I cannot say-
But give me an hour or so today-
And I've captured those minutes
With this craft I display!

118

## Mental Relief

My rosebud opened into bloom-
Unfolding petals pink, red, and
Maroon-
This time lapsed magic presents
For me-
A relief from daily monotony-
As I gaze and look at this
Majestic beauty-
Cares and woes evaporate
My boring duties!

## PAGES OF MY BOOK

The pages of my life
Are bound into a book.
Characters in this tome,
Are family, friends, and foe.
Each person, place, or thing,
Brings joy, mirth, and woe-
And at the end of day-
While editing- I say-
My book is not "Novel"-
But these characters have
Made my day!

## The Commander

Seconds, minutes, hours, days,
Weeks, months-
Time gives, time takes-
Adding years it takes away-
And as life slips quickly away-
That ticking clock commands
The day!

## HEADY VERSE

I have a little poem,
It's stuck up in my head.
To choose a proper meter,
Has given me some dread.
So now my little poem
Sits snugly there instead.

## Today's "Electro Society"

The co-dependent nature
Of society today,
Lists not a friendly greeting
Nor a smile on the way-
But hinges on "TRONICS",
That are Electro Micro-Wave.

## Nature's Gift

The free flow form of honey,
On toast this early morn-
Awakened sleepy taste buds-
And gave sweetness to a day
New borne-
This free flow form of honey-
A candy gift of nature,
Gives bees a hive-
Their Honey Dorm!

## Glowing Branches

Branches and twigs lit up with a glow-
Tree trunks all covered with ice
And snow-
As snuggly at home I watch this show-
But further than that, I know I must leave
This beauteous scene-
And pursue the roads with their
Perilous gleam-
Thankfully behind the sandpaper
Thrust, of dutiful road crews-
In their ice blasting trucks!

DOT OSIKA

## CONFUSION

My musings could sometimes amuse,
But beware I can also confuse-
These abilities come unannounced-
As I offer advice without price-
So the caveat I offer today,
Take heed of what I say-
As my musing is at play-
Leading you astray!

## Expressions

Poetical expression seeks
Words that spell it out-
Composed and put together,
It holds a lot of clout!

## Sea Oats

The sea oats ripening in the
Long summer's growth-
Bend and sway to the North East
Blow-
The sand dunes play the catcher's
Role-
And there in spring the oats unfold!

## March Geraniums

Don't die on me, oh my geranium,
For now in March I see your wilted
Leaves-
Don't die on me oh, my geranium-
For summer time your beauty
Needs-
Don't die on me oh, my geranium-
For bright and sunny vibes your
Blooms do bring!

## My Window Sill

There is this narrow platform.
The sets above the sink.
Upon it I place vases, and
Mementoes as I please.
I stand and do my dishes.
A mundane task each day.
It's then this narrow platform,
Becomes a stage for me.
The vases and mementoes,
Hold stories and set me free,
From boring tasks of washing dishes into
Thoughts of reveries.

## Nature's Video

The video of nature is on a
Constant run-
The sky, the beach, the ocean-
Present a full time spin-
If only with our vision, we willingly
Look in.

## Ocean Shore

The azure reflecting sea mirrors
an image of tranquility-
Seagulls soaring in the sky-
Gracefully pilot their weightless
Flight-
While ocean's ebbing tidal flow-
Widens the sandy tarmac below!

## January 2004

This January month of
Two thousand four
Was to me a complete bore!
As days slipped into nights
The landscape was a
Continual frozen bleak sight!

## Loosen Up

Feeling blue is not for you
So loosen up today
A happy face and a smile in place
Enough to erase
That frown on your face
As feeling blue is not for you
And as you loosen up today
And smile your troubles away
Don't let those blues descend on you.

## Birds of January

A communion of birds
Pecked furiously away
On this cold January day.
Thistle, corn, and sunflower seed,
Provided for them
A smorgasbord treat.
The Cardinal and mate as
If on a date,
Blue Jays and Finches and Juncos too. A commune of birds at my
Feeder today
Provided for me a bright
January Day!!

## Time Lapse

White buds in the sunshine
On this pleasant day of June
Ready for action
To reveal their petal blooms
In a short time lapse progression
Waving in the freeze
The Shasta Daisy's glory
Unfolds for us to see!

## Modern Cars

I am a senior citizen
With car memories of long ago
Autos of past eras were no great show
And now the sands of time
Have ushered in on stage
Performing cars currently the rage!
To engineers I say Hooray, Hooray
For setting on stage
The cars that perform in this play
With beauty comfort and ease
So as I drive my new Ford Focus
I am so very pleased!!!

## Rosebud Message

My rose bud a glorious red
It's stem and leaves support its head
Each morning ere the chores begin
This crimson beauty relates me
With words of silent mystery
Wake up and look about and see
Unfolding buds of life for you and me!

## Thankful Bites

An octogenarian thought one day
As she sat at breakfast and chewed away(????)
I can walk and talk (???) and do chores of the day
And as I chew and chew and chew away
I thank my molars, premolars, and incisors too
That these pearls for all these years have with me stayed.

## A Three Day Hunger

My birds, fair weather eaters are they,
As three day gales nest them away
And then the calm returns today.
Their three day hunger propels
Their wings to my feeder
Again and Again!

## Now That I am Old

Now that I am old,
My thought let me unfold.
My youth, a shy young me,
And cute as cute could be
Restraints on inner self
As many blushes I felt
And now, no longer shy
Good looks have passed me by
Tuffs of vanity, no longer a weight on me
And freer than I've ever been
Am glad that wisdom has set in.

## The Seeds of Weeds

The seeds of weeds, profuse indeed.
Outgrow the food I so much need.
The battles on in summer time.
My veggies grow row on row
These invaders of green
With aching back and hoe in hand.
I whack away.
These pests of land!

## Single Engine Pilots

An airport tarmac, in
My backyard.
Hosts feathered flying pilots
Darting in and out
No watch tower provided
For these single engine pilots
Command their flight precisely
And refueling at my station
Airborne they go
On auto-pilot!

## Sowing Wildness

The seasons come, the seasons go
And each its seeds of wildness sows.
Roadside landscapes flowers grow.
Some so pretty, some so, so.
And as these seasons come and go.
Varieties of people also grow.
Some so gentle and so kind.
Others wild and lack refine.
And so the seasons come and go,
As human beings still
Wildness sow!

## Food For A Day

A raptor sits there
In this tree,
As rigid as he could be.
Such patience and vigilance has he,
And then a swift and
Bull's eye shot.
He swoops to Earth
And on the spot.
Talons and beak hold his prey,
In securing our raptor
Food for a day!

## Famous Armor

The famous must wear any armor,
To protect them from verbal attacks.
Notoriety in this society
Keeps reporters right on track!
Newsprint, the wired and wireless,
Relentless in pursuit.
Shoot work bullets at their victims
At a merciless rate
Keeping alive the "Fourth Estate".

## A Rose Waltz

The rose bud did my vase engrace
Then slowly at its own pace
This bud began "The Flower Waltz"
Dressed in radiant colors of pinks
The petals unfurled
And bowed to me
Ending their "Flower Waltz"
Into a pretty pink bloom!

## Charged Battery

The days they come,
The days they go.
Making me older grow.
The past it came so very fast.
The future, one wonders
How long it will last?
But today am I
But today is today
Not yesterday.
I've charged my time battery
And go on with the show.

DOT OSIKA

## Katie's Flowers

Two yellows, one white.
Petals performing in sunlight.
Stems upright, shooting graceful
Bends of leaves.
Egg shaped, oval blooms, change form.
Tea cup now, with scalloped edge.
Fully opened, Tulip blooms.

## A Red Flash

It swooped through the air
With a vivid red glare
This flash gave alert to my
Senses inert.
In focus my eyes perceived
To be
The brightest red feathers
A Cardinal was He!!

## Radiant Beauty

Fall leaves with burst of color
Give radiant praise to God
Then humble of finite nature
Descend to earth replenishing next spring's birth

### Yellow Bird

My thistle seed feeder
As busy as it can be,
Is hosting Yellow Finches
Whose energy amazes me.
Straight, circular, vertical flights
Before on feeder alight.
These miniature birds of night
Zoom quickly out of my sight.

### History Reveals To Us

History reveals to us,
The foibles of mankind,
As lust for power in ages past
Remains with us very steadfast.
Battlefields change in our time
As wars are waged on currency grounds.
The CEO'S as lusty as can be
Us ammunition to
Diminish you and me!

### Cardinal

A red Cardinal on a gray winter's day
Brightens my spirit on this gloomy day

## Karats In The Sun

T'was early Wednesday midmorning
At nine to be sure.
When August rain storm
Left dripping oh so pure.
Refracted by the sun rays
These glistening droplets displayed
The purity of diamonds
But quickly dried away!!

## A Heavy Journey

The journey, so heavy
Beyond belief
My Mate has died and left me grief
I trudge along this lonely path
So burdened down with memories past
The pace so slow
The thoughts so fast
With events of a happier past
And now as near the Journey's end
It's time I shed my grief and said,
"Life is sweet and I'll trudge ahead!"

## It's Wake Up Time

This "Frost is on the Pumpkin" morning
Take heed, this is a warning.
The icy sparkles sparkling,
Not diamonds to be sure.
Their captivating beauty
Is a gradual enhancing lure
Into snowy, frozen vistas galore.

## Winter Past

Dull drab grays of winter past
Enough is enough this cannot last
And so into their closets on this
First day of Spring
Where vast range of colors all winter spent
These dull drab frays in their silent ways
Donned a vast palette of shades
And presented to us
A spring time landscape
So dainty and fresh forgiving the dull drab
Grays of winter past.

## My P.C. Guide

There is this P.C. inside of me
Director and guidance it offers free.
Do this!  Do that!  Arise and shine!
It's then the inner self of me
Obeys the programmed P.C.
The arms they swing, the legs they walk
The mind so chipper with chips inside
Looks clearly to this P.C. guide!

## Nature's Lab

On this hot August day
I perspire away
The hedgerow with its lofty trees
Provides this cool refreshing breeze
As nature conditions the air I breathe
The temp is 80:  humidity high
My sun deck shaded and here sit I
Grateful for these merciful trees
Their beauty silent each one a lab performing chemistry:
for free for Man!

## October Birds

The birds at my feeder
This October day
Are pecking, pecking and pecking away.
Blue Jays assertively use their sway
Keeping Chickadees and Titmouse and Sparrows at bay.
But soon my little friends clever are they
Out with the Blue Jays between bites
And my feeder gives
Me a bird watchers delight!

## A Constant Pace

Time with its consistent pace
Has us running a frantic race
Duties galore, appointments met
A sigh of relief, but it's not over yet!
As the hands of the clock
Still in command
A new day is born
Tired and forlorn
We lessen our pace
Letting time win the race!

## God's Little Angels

God's little angels of flight
On this a cold sunny November day
The perching birds are pecking away
The thistle, corn, and sunflower seeds
Supply these aviators the fuel they need.
And so God's little **angels** of flight
Provide shear delight!

## Time

Time with its consistent pace
Has us running a frantic pace
Duties galore-appointments met
A sigh of relief but it's not over yet
As the hands o' the clock still in command
A new day is born
Tired and forlorn
We lessen our pace
Letting time win the race!

## A Fleeting Delight

Amorphous as they glide on high
We catch their beauty with a sigh
As Turner, Moore and artists galore
Painted and painted these billowing fluffs
Red, orange, silver, and grayish white
Stratus or nimbus such a
Fleeting delight!

## Old Age Parade

As I march along in this old age parade
My step through not steady, determination strong
Fellow paraders advanced in years
Carry canes and limbs insecure
Faces etched by merciless time
We join this parade
With memories so dear
And Happy to have lived another year

## Chips

I feel chipper today!
The computer beckons unto me -
So let the chips fall where ever
They may!

## Seedy Pleasure

Late February: early March
As winter sheds its snows
It's then the urge within
Beckons me to begin
An assemblage of various tins
Cottage cheese, yogurt whatever
Home to my seeds dried treasure
Erupting in May for my pleasure!

## TV or not TV

Flipping my TV channels reveal much to me
My cable TV channels
TV or not TV
That is the question I ask me!
Drug ads disclose such symptoms
That put a fright in me
TV or not TV
That is the question
Drugs, politics, economics are enough to make me sick!!

## Bed

Early this January morn
My bed is nice and warm
It's then my inner engine refuses to perform
The mind a powerful ignition key
Starts priming ideas to me!
And slowly as I leave this cozy nest
The engine revs
I leave this bed

## New Book

As I sit, a new book in hand
Flipping pages
Offers and inside look
Mysteries other wise untold
Romances of ages
Verbally unfold
These pages one by one
Hold my wonderment in command

DOT OSIKA

## Recycled Glory

Autumnal glory, colors galore
Summers landscape, robed in green
Bowing to approaching time
Whimsically changes its verdant robe
Donning flirtations autumnal colors
Teasing a viewers awesome delight
Unaware of time's plan
To limit its life
And fall to Earth as recycled glory!

## Flipping My T.V. Channels

T.V. or not T.V.
Reveal too much to me!
Drug ads disclose such symptoms
That put a fright in me!
So it's T.V. or not T.V.?
That is the question!
As drugs, politics, economics
Are enough to make me sick.

## **<u>Lawn Alert!</u>**

My lawn it looked sufficiently
Green-
Save for the forest, I did not see
The trees!
Till suddenly on channel three,
A gardening specialist alerted
Me!
"The lawn so green isn't what
You perceive it to be!"
Said he.
The sheep sorrel, dandelions,
Chickweed and clover-
And also plantains and burdock,
Take over-
So now as I look around,
Invaders of green on my lawn,
Abound-
With aching back, and hoe in hand-
I whack away at these invaders
Of land.